D1567919

Rookie Read-About® Science

It Could Still Be A Leaf

By Allan Fowler

Consultants:
Robert L. Hillerich, Professor Emeritus,
Bowling Green State University, Bowling Green, Ohio
Consultant, Pinellas County Schools, Florida

Lynn Kepler, Educational Consultant

Fay Robinson, Child Development Specialist

CHILDRENS PRESS®
CHICAGO

E
Fow
ccL
12/94
14.40

Library of Congress Cataloging-in-Publication Data

Fowler, Allan.
    It Could Still be a leaf / by Allan Fowler.
      p. cm — (Rookie read-about science.)
      Summary: Discusses different kinds of leaves, the forms and colors
they may have, and their function.
      ISBN 0-516-06017-1
      1. Leaves—Juvenile literature. [1. Leaves.] I. Title.
    II. Series: Fowler, Allan. Rookie read-about science.
QK649.F68 1993
581.1'0427—dc20   93-882
                                               CIP
                                               AC

All the world looks green and fresh in summer, when the trees are covered with green leaves.

But a leaf could be red or
golden yellow,

. . . and still be a leaf.

Many leaves change color in the
fall from green to red or yellow.
These autumn leaves are beautiful

8

When winter comes,
leaves of many kinds of
trees drop to the ground —

and the branches are bare.

These trees stay bare until spring, when buds swell on the branches.

Tiny new leaves unfold from the buds.

They grow in the sunlight.

Some trees, such as oaks and maples, have a single leaf on each stem.

Other trees have several
leaflets on each stem, like
the ash tree.

Leaves could be big and floppy,
like those on palm trees,

. . . and still be leaves.

They could be narrow, like the leaves of a weeping willow.

Or they could be slender
needles on pine trees or . . .

giant sequoias,
and still be
leaves.

Trees such as pines are called evergreens. Their needles stay green all year round.

Almost all plants have leaves.

Vines, bushes, and flowering
plants have leaves.

Did you know that you often
walk on leaves, or fields of
leaves? You do! Because
each blade of grass is a leaf.

Something could be good to eat and still be a leaf, like lettuce or cabbage or spinach.

All the food we eat comes from plants or from animals that eat plants.

Leaves help plants grow.

Every leaf takes in light
from the sun to make food
for its plant.

At the same time, the leaf
gives out oxygen.

People need oxygen to
breathe, and most oxygen
comes from the leaves
on trees.

So leaves are needed for life
on Earth.

They do something else
for us, too.

On a hot, sunny day,
we can sit in the shade
of a leafy tree.

It's a nice, cool place to be.

29

Words You Know

summer   autumn   winter   spring

oak   maple   ash

branches   buds   new leaves

palm trees

weeping willow

needles

pine trees

giant sequoias

flowering plants

grass

Index

About the Author

Allan Fowler is a free-lance writer with a background in advertising. Born in New York, he lives in Chicago now and enjoys traveling.

Photo Credits

SuperStock International, Inc. – ©Gary Neil Corbett, Cover; ©Tom Rosenthal, 3, 30 (top left), 18, 31 (center center), 22; ©Mauritius, 6; ©Pablo Rivera, 21, 31 (bottom center); ©George Glod, 24; ©David Spindel, 25; © Joel Degere, 29

Valan – ©Dr. A. Farquhar, 4; ©John Cancalosi, 5; ©Kennon Cooke, 7, 12, 15, 19, 30, (top left center, top right center, center left), 31, (top right); ©Alan Wilkinson, 8, 30 (bottom left); © Harold V. Green, 10, 30 (bottom center); ©J.R. Page, 11, 30 (top right, bottom right); ©Chris L. Gotman, 13, 30 (center right); ©A.B. Joyce, 14, 31 (top center); ©Albert Kuhnigk, 16, 31 (center right); ©V. Wilkinson, 17, 31 (left); ©K. Ghani, 20; ©S.J. Krasemann, 23, 31 (bottom right); ©Jean Bruneau, 27, 30 (center center)

COVER: Leaves